CHAPTER 1

THE NUTS AND BOLTS

In the digital marketing panorama, affiliate marketing is a standout model. Here, a symbiotic relationship forms between businesses (or merchants) and promoters, which can be individuals or organizations (referred to as affiliates). The objective is simple: endorse the merchants' products or services, and get paid for every successful conversion achieved from these promotional campaigns. Affiliate marketing is a mutual win: merchants grow their customer base, increase revenue, and only pay for fruitful results. Affiliates, conversely, earn profits minus the challenges of manufacturing products, managing stock, or dealing with customer service.

THE MECHANICS OF AFFILIATE MARKETING: A DETAILED LOOK

Before diving into affiliate marketing, it's essential to understand its core mechanism.

Here's a step-by-step breakdown:

Affiliates align themselves with an affiliate program or network that hosts an array of merchants.

Affiliates handpick the products or services they want to champion and receive unique affiliate links. These links carry tracking data to ensure the proper credit of sales.

Using these exclusive affiliate links, affiliates promote the chosen products or services across various platforms like websites, blogs, social media, email newsletters, and more.

As soon as a visitor clicks on an affiliate link and carries out the desired action (such as buying a product or subscribing to a newsletter), it's tracked and recorded by the affiliate program or network.

The affiliate earns a commission based on the agreed rate for every successful action (sale, lead, or others).

The affiliate program or network distributes the earned commissions to affiliates, typically every month or once a minimum threshold is met.

Affiliate marketing generally encompasses four key models:

Pay-per-sale (PPS): The most common model where you earn a commission each time a referral from you makes a purchase from the merchant.

Pay-per-lead (PPL): This model rewards

you for generating potential leads for the merchant. A commission is earned whenever a visitor you referred carries out a specified action, such as signing up for a newsletter.

Pay-per-click (PPC): You earn for driving traffic to the merchant's website, regardless of whether the visitor purchases anything.

Multi-tier affiliate marketing: This variant allows you to earn commissions on your referrals and the referrals made by affiliates you recruited.

THE APPEAL OF AFFILIATE MARKETING

Over the years, affiliate marketing has solidified its place as a popular choice for both novice and seasoned marketers. Here are a few reasons:

Minimal startup costs: Affiliate marketing can be started with a basic website or blog, which can be set up with a small investment.

Flexibility and scalability: Affiliate marketing allows you to operate at a pace that suits you. You can scale your efforts to elevate your income potential as your audience grows.

Passive income potential: Once your promotional strategies and high-quality content are in place, affiliate marketing can provide a steady income flow.

Performance-based rewards: Your earnings are tied directly to your efforts. The more conversions you drive, the higher your income.

Wide product selection: Affiliate marketing offers a broad spectrum of products and services to promote, enabling you to pick offers that resonate with your target audience.

Global market reach: Affiliate marketing provides a platform to cater to consumers worldwide.

No product creation needed: You can promote other companies' products or services, saving you time and effort.

Low risk: Since you're not responsible for product development, inventory, or customer support, affiliate marketing is a relatively risk-free venture.

In summary, affiliate marketing presents a golden opportunity for those seeking to step into the digital entrepreneurship space. To truly succeed, it's essential to lay a solid groundwork. As we proceed to the next chapter, "Building the Framework," we'll delve into the initial steps required to establish a successful affiliate marketing venture. This includes topics like selecting a lucrative niche, identifying your target audience, and studying market trends and competitors.

Embarking on your affiliate marketing journey, we aim to equip you with the necessary knowledge and tools for a flourishing enterprise. Let's step confidently into the world of affiliate marketing!

CHAPTER 2

THE ART OF FOCUSING YOUR SCOPE

"Trying to cater to everyone often leads to reaching no one." This business philosophy accentuates the importance of honing in on a particular consumer group for your products or services. Striving to please every potential customer dilutes your brand message and causes misalignment with your audience. People have unique needs, wants, and preferences; a catch-all marketing approach doesn't resonate with the vast majority. On the contrary, successful marketing involves understanding a specific consumer segment, immersing yourself in their problems, and tailoring your message to solve their issues directly. This method creates a strong connection with your potential clients and boosts the likelihood of transforming them into steadfast supporters.

For example, if you're promoting a groundbreaking meditation cushion, marketing it to every meditation enthusiast might appear tempting. However, refining your target market to beginners in meditation who value extra support and comfort in a meditation cushion can assist you in crafting a compelling and more impactful message, thereby elevating your prospects of success. Thus, defining a focused segment is an essential initial stride in establishing a firm foundation for your affiliate marketing endeavor.

WHAT IS A FOCUSED SEGMENT?

Picture a focused segment as a targeted area of interest within a larger market, a unique portion you will cater to with your content and promotions. Identifying a focused segment lets you zero in on a specific group of individuals with similar interests, problems, or needs.

But why is this pivotal in affiliate marketing? Here are a few reasons:

Firstly, it allows you to create content that directly addresses your potential customers' desires and requirements, simplifying the process of building trust and credibility—both are vital in a prosperous affiliate marketing endeavor.

Secondly, it aids in differentiating you from competitors. A unique approach tailored to a specific audience will help you differentiate, attract a committed following, and enhance your odds of long-term success.

To better understand this concept, let's take a look at some examples of focused segments:

Healthy Eating: This sector is broad. You can hone in on something like "Plant-based diets for athletes," offering specialized content and products for athletes looking to maintain or improve their performance through plant-based nutrition.

Travel & Adventure: This is another large market with numerous sub-segments. You might specialize in "Eco-conscious travel for solo travelers," providing tips, hacks, and suggestions for single travelers aiming to explore the world sustainably.

Sustainable Living: Instead of targeting all eco-conscious consumers, you could choose a segment like "Zero waste living for small households," sharing insights, strategies, and product recommendations for small families seeking to reduce their waste and environmental footprint.

As these examples illustrate, a focused segment is a narrower part of a larger market. When deciding on a segment, you should consider your personal interests, the segment's potential profitability, competitiveness, and audience size.

IDENTIFYING A FOCUSED SEGMENT

Choosing the right focused segment is a pivotal decision in your affiliate marketing journey. It will guide the kind of products or services you endorse, the content you produce, and the audience you cater to. Here are some aspects to consider when identifying a segment for your affiliate marketing enterprise:

Personal passion and interest: It's significantly easier to generate engaging content and recommend products in a sector that genuinely intrigues you. An impassioned connection with your chosen segment makes your content more believable, authentic, and keeps you energized in the long run.

Profitability: While a passion for your chosen segment is vital, it's equally important to ensure it has the potential to generate income. Investigate the affiliate programs available within your chosen segment to verify there is ample demand for the products or services you plan to promote.

Competitiveness: Assessing the competitiveness of your chosen segment helps understand the level of market saturation. Some competition is advantageous as it confirms market demand for the products and services you plan to promote. However, an overly competitive segment can make it difficult to distinguish yourself and gain momentum.

Audience Size and Engagement: A sizable and engaged audience is essential for a thriving affiliate marketing enterprise. Evaluating the size and engagement of your target audience within your segment is another way to ensure there's sufficient demand for the content and products you'll be promoting.

In conclusion, identifying the right focused segment for your affiliate marketing venture is a vital step. Thoughtful consideration of your personal interests, segment profitability, competitiveness, and audience size will guide you in choosing a segment that aligns with your passions and promises to generate income.

CHAPTER 3

FORGING YOUR ONLINE PRESENCE AND DIGITAL HUB

In the world of affiliate marketing, your online presence is the ambassador of your ideas and work. This presence is often anchored in your website or blog, a digital stage for content sharing, promoting affiliate items, and fostering connections with your audience.

Selecting Your Virtual Canvas: The first step in crafting your website is selecting the ideal platform. Numerous options such as WordPress, Squarespace, Wix, and Joomla are available, each with their own pros and cons. Considerations such as ease of use, flexibility in design, and growth potential should influence your decision. WordPress often wins favor due to its versatility, vast plugin selection, and supportive community, making it an appealing option for beginners and seasoned users alike.

Identifying Your Domain Name: A domain

name (like www.example.com) is the online street address for your website. It should be memorable, easy to type, and resonate with your niche. Ideally, it should include keywords that are relevant to your target audience. Domain names can be secured through registrars such as Google Domains, Namecheap, or GoDaddy. For instance, if you're focusing on "sustainable living practices", a domain like "ecoconsciouslife.com" might be a good fit.

Here's a brief guide on how to secure a domain name:

A. Idea Generation: Kick off the process by brainstorming a list of potential domain names that are unique, tied to your niche, and simple to spell.

B. Availability Check: Use the search tool provided by most domain registrars to see if your preferred domain name is free for use.

C. Registrar Selection: Opt for a domain registrar that aligns with your needs and budget. GoDaddy and Google Domains are popular choices, and some CMS platforms also allow direct domain purchase.

D. Account Creation: Set up an account with your chosen registrar by providing the necessary personal details.

E. Purchase: Once you've found an available domain name, go ahead and secure it. Registrars typically offer various registration lengths and additional features like privacy protection or email services.

F. Payment: Enter your payment information to finalize the purchase.

G. Email Verification: Once you've made the purchase, you'll need to verify your email address to keep your domain active.

With your domain in hand, the following steps involve selecting a web hosting service and getting your website up and running.

Choosing a Web Hosting Service: Web hosting is what makes your website accessible on the internet. Providers such as HostGator, SiteGround, and Bluehost offer a variety of plans to suit different needs. When choosing a hosting provider, take into account factors like performance, dependability, customer service, and pricing.

Tailoring Your Website: With your platform, domain, and hosting in place, you can install your CMS and start customizing your website. Core pages such as Home, About, Contact, and Privacy Policy & Disclaimer should be set up before you start crafting content. Once the basic structure is in place, you're ready to create engaging and valuable content for your audience.

Aside from your website, you can harness other online platforms like Instagram, Pinterest, YouTube, Facebook, and email marketing to broaden your reach and boost your affiliate products. Collaborations with influencers and bloggers or using paid advertising options can also help expand your audience base.

Consistently generating high-quality, valuable content is the linchpin for success in affiliate marketing. By understanding and addressing your audience's needs with insightful articles, product reviews, and step-by-step guides, you can build credibility and loyalty among your followers.

In summary, your website or blog is the cornerstone of your online identity for affiliate marketing. While this chapter is quite dense with information, the aim is to equip you with the foundational knowledge you need to establish a robust online presence.

CHAPTER 4

MASTERING THE ART OF AFFILIATE PROGRAM

You've nailed down your niche, identified your ideal audience, and established your online persona. Now it's time to immerse yourself in the universe of affiliate programs. In this section, we'll help you navigate through commission models and rates to ensure that you are partnering with the optimal affiliate programs for your business venture.

There's no universal solution when it comes to commission rates. Each program provides different commission models, making it crucial to comprehend your alternatives and balance the advantages and drawbacks of each.

Generally, you'll encounter three common types:

Percentage-based Commissions: In this model, your earnings are a proportion of the sale price of each product or service you endorse. Imagine you're in the fashion arena and join a program that provides a 10% commission rate. If a customer purchases a $100 dress via your affiliate link, you pocket $10.

Flat-rate Commissions: Here, your earnings are a predetermined sum for each sale, regardless of the product's price. Let's say you advertise a software subscription offering a flat-rate commission of $30 per sale; you earn $30 each time someone subscribes via your affiliate link.

Tiered Commissions: Certain affiliate programs employ a tiered commission model where your commission rate escalates as you hit specific sales benchmarks. You might start with a 5% commission rate, which elevates to 10% after achieving 50 sales.

Now, let's explore factors to consider when analyzing commission rates and structures.

Average Order Value (AOV): The AOV refers to the typical expenditure by a customer on a purchase. When evaluating affiliate programs, it's critical to consider how AOV might affect your earnings. For instance, a high commission rate on a low-priced item might not be as lucrative as a lower commission rate on a more expensive product. Let's examine this with a hypothetical example:

Program A offers a 15% commission on products with an AOV of $50, and Program B offers a 5% commission on products with an AOV of $300. If you generate 10 sales through each program, your earnings from Program A would be $75, while those from Program B would be $150.

As illustrated, despite Program A offering a higher commission rate, the lower AOV leads to lesser earnings than Program B.

Customer Lifetime Value (CLV): Some affiliate programs provide recurring commissions for subscription-based products or services, allowing you to earn a commission for every payment a customer makes. CLV refers to the total revenue a business anticipates earning from a single customer over the duration of their relationship. This can be especially rewarding if the customers you refer have a high CLV and continue their subscription for several months or even years.

Earning Potential: Reflect on the earning potential of the affiliate program based on your niche, target audience, and the products or services you intend to endorse.

Conversion Rates: A program with a high commission rate won't be profitable if the products or services are challenging to sell. Hunt for programs with a proven track record of high conversion rates and customer satisfaction.

Dive into ClickBank: Numerous affiliate platforms are available for exploration, but ClickBank stands out as a prominent and popular affiliate marketing platform. Here's a quick rundown on how to kickstart your journey with ClickBank:

Registration on ClickBank: Visit the ClickBank website and finish the registration process. You will gain access to your dashboard, where you can search for products and track your performance. Product Selection: Use your ClickBank account to search for products related to your niche in the Marketplace.

Understanding Gravity Scores: ClickBank assigns a Gravity score to each product, which reflects the number of successful sales made by affiliates in the last 12 weeks. A higher Gravity score typically suggests better conversion rates.

Evaluate Sales Pages: Before endorsing a product, review its sales page as it can impact conversion rates significantly.

Promotion and Performance Tracking: After selecting a product, start promoting it using your unique affiliate link.

UNDERSTANDING COOKIE DURATION AND TRACKING IN AFFILIATE MARKETING

Cookies in affiliate marketing are small text files that store information about a user's online activity.

When a user clicks on your affiliate link, a cookie gets placed on their device, enabling the affiliate program to track the user's actions on the advertiser's website.

Cookie duration or "cookie life" refers to the time a cookie remains active on a user's device after they click on your affiliate link. This duration can vary from a few days to several months, depending on the affiliate program. Longer durations increase the probability of earning commissions, especially in industries with longer sales cycles, such as travel or high-ticket items.

REPUTATION OF PRODUCT AND MERCHANT: A KEY CONSIDERATION

The reputation of the product and the merchant is a vital factor when choosing affiliate programs. Endorse high-quality products from reputable merchants to earn your audience's trust and

CHAPTER 5

EFFECTIVE STORYTELLING

Embarking on the journey of affiliate marketing requires a deep understanding of the products you're promoting. This comprehension lays the foundation for engaging content that piques the interest of your potential customers, converting them into regular buyers. Here's a breakdown of how you can communicate the allure of your products through captivating reviews and enticing narratives.

Research is key:

Before diving headfirst into product reviews, arm yourself with detailed information about the product. Learn about the pros, cons, features, and any potential glitches. It would be even more advantageous if you could get hands-on experience with the product. For instance, if you're advocating for a new skincare range, use it for some time to witness its effects. Noticing a change, be it positive or negative, will lead to a more genuine review. In the instance where you come across an appealing product with a lucrative commission but it fails to deliver as promised, be honest. Transparency with your audience about your experiences will enhance the authenticity of your endorsements.

The Power of a Strong Opening: Set the tone of your review with a compelling introduction. Give a snapshot of the product, its standout features, and the aspects you'll be covering in your review. Sharing a personal story or the reason behind choosing the product will create a bond with the readers. For instance, instead of beginning with "Are you tired of fitness trackers that promise the world but fall short on performance? I was too." opt for "Ever felt betrayed by the exaggerated claims of fitness gadgets? Join the club! My experiment with the FitTrack Pro is an interesting tale of discovery and realization, which I'm excited to share."

A Feature-Focused Breakdown:

Structure your review into easily digestible sections. Discuss the features of the product and how they can add value to the reader's life. Adopt a user-friendly format with subheadings, bullet points, and short paragraphs to facilitate easy reading. So, instead of a section titled "Design and Comfort," use "Aesthetics and the Comfort Quotient".

Tackling Drawbacks:

Highlight any limitations or issues you encountered with the product. This honesty will create trust between you and your readers and make your review more balanced. For instance, if you found the initial setup of FitTrack Pro a bit tricky, let your readers know about it and provide potential solutions if possible.

Personalize Your Experience:

Add a dash of personal experience to your review. Sharing your likes and dislikes about the product, and its impact on your life, adds a personal touch to the narrative. This connection will help your readers envision the product's effect on their own lives.

Wrap Up with a Call-to-Action:

Conclude with a brief summary of your thoughts about the product. Clearly state your recommendation and the reasons behind it. End with a call-to-action prompting the readers to click your affiliate link if they're intrigued by the product.

A Picture is Worth a Thousand Words:

Visual representation can be a great tool to make your review more engaging. Include high-quality images or videos of the product from different perspectives and demonstrate its usage, if possible.

Honesty is the Best Policy:

Maintain an unbiased, honest approach throughout the review. Your readers will value your integrity, and this trust will go a long way in building a loyal audience for your affiliate marketing.

The Art of Storytelling:

Incorporate your personal journey, challenges, and victories related to the product in the review. This narrative will resonate with your readers on a deeper level.

Engage Your Readers:

Encourage your readers to share their thoughts or experiences about the product. This engagement will create a sense of community and provide additional perspectives to the readers.

CHAPTER 6

AMPLIFYING YOUR PARTNER MARKETING VENTURE

In this chapter, we unveil the secrets of amplifying your partner marketing venture. A successful venture's key lies in not putting all your eggs in one basket, or in other words, creating a mosaic of revenue streams. By doing this, you cushion your business against unforeseen risks while enhancing your potential earnings. We'll delve into different ways to enrich this mosaic and guide you through real-life applications for your own partner marketing expedition. Let's ascend to the next level!

LAYING THE FOUNDATION FOR EXPANSION

Diversify Your Affiliate Portfolio:

Depending on a single or a couple of affiliate programs may hinder your earnings and expose you to unpredictable policy changes. An antidote to this is expanding your portfolio to include a spectrum of products or services in your specialized field. This way, even if one program underperforms or folds, you have other sources to rely on. For instance, a travel-focused marketer could endorse a wide range of services like accommodation booking platforms, airline aggregators, travel insurance, and even travel equipment.

Blend in Display Advertising:

Even though your central focus might be affiliate marketing, integrating display ads can offer a steady side income.

Services like Google AdSense, Media.net, or Ezoic allow you to host ads on your site and earn based on impressions or clicks. However, ensure your site doesn't get swamped with ads, as it can sour the user experience.

Develop and Market Proprietary Products:

As you cultivate your audience and establish your authority in your field, contemplate developing and selling proprietary products like ebooks, courses, or even tangible goods. This not only adds a new income stream but also grants you more business control. For instance, a fitness blogger could curate personalized workout regimes, nutrition guides, or even launch a line of fitness gear.

Dispense Specialist Services or Coaching:

Your specialized knowledge can be a gold mine. Monetize it by offering consulting or coaching services. This not only enriches your income stream but allows you to connect with your audience on a deeper level. For example, a marketing maven could conduct personal coaching sessions or group workshops to empower small business owners to boost their digital footprint.

Remember, the secret ingredient to success is being adaptable and fostering continuous growth.

BUILDING YOUR A-TEAM AND DELEGATING

As your partner marketing venture expands, you may find it increasingly difficult to manage all operations single-handedly. Building a reliable team and delegating tasks can be a game-changer.

Deciphering Delegable Tasks:

Identify tasks that can be outsourced – tasks that might be too time-consuming, require specialized knowledge, or simply aren't your strong suit. In affiliate marketing, such tasks can include content creation, graphic design, social media management, email marketing, or website administration.

Set a Budget:

Determine a comfortable budget for outsourcing before starting your hiring process. You can set a monthly or project-based budget, based on the nature of the tasks. Always prioritize quality over cost – remember, the least expensive choice might not yield the desired results.

Engage the Perfect Freelancers or Agencies:

Platforms like Upwork, Freelancer, and Fiverr are treasure troves of skilled freelancers. You can also delve into niche-specific job boards or reach out to your professional network. While shortlisting candidates, consider their experience, expertise, communication skills, and previous client feedback.

Test the Waters:

Assign a small paid task before finalizing any long-term commitment. This allows you to evaluate their skills, work ethics, and adherence to deadlines.

Set Clear Expectations:

Share your expectations, project timelines, communication preferences, and goals with your team. Providing them with a clear brief and being open to queries ensures they fully understand your needs.

Supervise Progress and Provide Feedback:

Regularly review your team's work and offer constructive feedback. Regular check-ins ensure your team aligns with your expectations.

Adapt and Expand Your Team:

As your venture grows, you may need to expand your team or hire additional freelancers with unique skills. Regularly evaluate your team's performance and your business needs to make necessary adjustments.

VENTURING INTO UNCHARTED TERRITORIES

Once you've built a robust partner marketing venture in one field, consider venturing into new fields. Here are some strategies to help you broaden your horizon while maintaining your current success.

Identify Potential New Fields:

Research new fields that align with your interests, expertise, and market potential. Look for fields that have a growing audience, ample products or services to promote, and affiliate programs with enticing commission rates.

Evaluate Market Demand and Competition:

Before foraying into a new field, analyze the market demand and competition. Use tools like Google Trends and keyword research tools to determine if there's an adequate audience and scope for growth.

CHAPTER 7

MASTERING THE AFFILIATE SYMPHONY

Performance Insights, Experimentation,
and Collaborative Bonds

In the grand orchestra of affiliate marketing, achieving mastery requires a harmonious blend of performance tracking, creative experimentation, and fostering strong alliances with partners. This chapter unveils the secrets to elevate your affiliate marketing endeavors to extraordinary heights.

Section 1: Unveiling the Power of Performance Tracking and Optimization

To unlock the full potential of affiliate marketing, equip yourself with the tools to measure and optimize your performance. Embrace the world of analytics and conversion tracking, leading you to data-driven decisions and remarkable results.

1.1 Igniting Insights with Google Analytics

Empower yourself with the formidable tool of Google Analytics to gain valuable metrics, from visitor count to bounce rate. Unravel the process of setting up Google Analytics on your website, and embrace the clarity of audience behavior and preferences.

1.2 The Journey Through Affiliate-Specific Tracking

Navigate the landscape of affiliate-specific tracking systems to monitor clicks, conversions, and commissions. Diversify your toolkit by exploring tracking tools unique to the affiliate programs you

AFFILIATE MASTERY: UNLEASHING THE SYMPHONY OF SUCCESS

work with, such as Amazon Associates Central.

1.3 Precision in Conversion Tracking

Implement precision tracking mechanisms to attribute conversions to specific sources or campaigns. Optimize your marketing initiatives for higher efficiency and ROI, measuring campaign effectiveness through platforms like Google Ads.

1.4 UTM Parameters: Illuminating Your Campaign Universe

Discover the power of UTM parameters, adding tags to affiliate links to track marketing channels and campaigns.

Unveil the origins and effectiveness of your traffic, shaping your strategies for maximum impact.

1.5 A/B Testing: Crafting the Masterpiece of Optimization

Unlock creative experimentation with A/B testing,

comparing variations of elements to identify the best-performing ones. Let tools like Google Optimize guide your journey to evolution and optimization.

Section 2: Decoding Performance Metrics for Strategic Advantage

Decode the language of performance metrics, the keys to success. Gain mastery over clicks, conversion rates, EPC, ROI, and bounce rate through compelling examples.

2.1 Clicks: The Bridge to Audience Engagement

Master the art of monitoring click-through rates to understand the effectiveness of your content and promotions. Explore the significance of clicks through insightful examples.

2.2 Conversion Rate: Unraveling the Conversion Enigma

Unleash the potential of the conversion rate, understanding

the efficacy of your content, landing pages, and strategies.

2.3 Earnings Per Click (EPC): The Profitability Compass

Navigate the seas of profitability with EPC, comparing the performance of different programs and identifying lucrative traffic sources.

2.4 Return on Investment (ROI): The Journey to Profitability

Embark on a journey of profitability, measuring the success of your campaigns in generating revenue beyond costs.

2.5 Bounce Rate: The Measure of User Engagement

Uncover insights into user behavior and engagement through the bounce rate, optimizing content and user experience.

Section 3: Orchestrating Triumph Through A/B Testing and Nurturing Relationships

Seize the final chapters of triumph through A/B testing and building collaborative bonds with partners.

3.1 A/B Testing: The Art of Creative Refinement

Empower your strategies with A/B testing, identifying and refining elements to optimize performance.

3.2 Building Collaborative Bonds: The Key to Sustainable Success

Nurture collaborative relationships with partners through open communication, transparency, feedback, and industry networking.

In conclusion, your path to affiliate marketing excellence lies in the synergy of performance analysis, creative experimentation, and nurturing collaborative bonds. Embrace data-driven strategies and a deep understanding of performance metrics, continually refining your approach through A/B testing. Forge strong partnerships for sustainable success in the dynamic world of affiliate marketing.